Best. Journal. Ever.

by Max Brallier

PSS!
PRICE STERN SLOAN

An Imprint of Penguin Group (USA) LLC

PRICE STERN SLOAN
Published by the Penguin Group
Penguin Group (USA) LLC, 375 Hudson Street, New York, New York 10014, USA

USA | Canada | UK | Ireland | Australia | New Zealand | India | South Africa | China

penguin.com
A Penguin Random House Company

Published in 2013 by Price Stern Sloan, a division of Penguin Young Readers Group,
345 Hudson Street, New York, New York 10014. PSS! is a registered trademark of
Penguin Group (USA) LLC. Printed in the U.S.A.

ISBN 978-0-8431-7801-2   10 9 8 7 6 5 4 3 2 1

Skips

Benson

Mordecai

Skips's cousin Quips tells the absolute **worst** jokes. But bad jokes are sometimes kind of the best jokes. Write down the worst jokes you know—or come up with some new ones.

yo mamaso
farherfous
useciodeworme

WHY DID tHe CLOWN gO to tHe DOCtOR? He WAS FeeLING a LIttLe FUNNY!

Mordecai and Rigby are serious slackers. They'll do **anything** to get out of doing crummy Park work. Wouldn't you?

Circle one!

Would you rather rake leaves for **three** hours or lick **three** toilet bowls?

Would you rather set up **five hundred** chairs or eat **five hundred** hard-boiled eggs?

Would you rather mow the **entire** Park lawn or spend the **entire** day at school with no pants on?

Would you rather **pick up** roadkill or **cuddle** roadkill?

Low Five Ghost once turned Mordecai
and Rigby into ghosts, and the dudes
had to scare a bunch of their peeps.
Scare some of your buddies, then
record their reactions below.

How you scared them:

Reaction:

How you scared them:

Reaction:

Mordecai and Rigby hosted a scary-movie night and showed the creepy classic **Zombocalypse 3-D.** Come up with your own idea for a 3-D horror movie.

What's the title?

sonic zombie

Who are the main characters?

sonic and rails

Where is it set?

yotube

Who's the bad guy?

zombies

What's the scariest part of the movie?

zombs

zombies showed up to our movie night.

Yeah, and Rigby was all terrified.

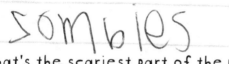

Draw a poster for your movie!

Mordecai and Rigby are best buds.
Mordecai is a blue jay, and Rigby is a
raccoon. Draw blue-jay and raccoon
versions of you and your best bud
below.

Rigby almost never loses at rock-paper-scissors. Grab a friend and have your own rock-paper-scissors showdown. How many can you win in a row? Record what happens below.

It's an evil game!

Mordecai and Rigby tried to show a thawed-out caveman what modern life was all about. It did not go well . . .

What would you tell a caveman about your modern life?

DUDe, I'm going to kill you.

Mordecai and Rigby are best buds, but that doesn't mean they don't annoy the heck out of each other sometimes.

What does your best friend do that **really** annoys you?

They talk to much

What do you do that **really** annoys your best friend?

being stupid *Some times*

What else **really** annoys both of you?

Rigby once unleashed a horde of evil hot dogs. What if **your** favorite food came to life and was all monstrous and evil? Draw it here!

Muscle Man is a serious prankster. He even defeated the rival East Pines Park in an epic prank war. Prank your buds and record their reactions here:

Prank:

How it went down:

Prank:

How it went down:

Prank:

How it went down:

Prank:

How it went down:

YOU KNOW WHO I PRANKED LAST NIGHT? MY MOM!

Dude, Fill in the Blanks!

Mordecai and Rigby are playing **Knife Bandit** when Benson tells them to set up the chairs. Mordecai asks Benson why he's such a huge tool. Uh-oh. Benson's face gets bright red, and he **freaks out** and screams, "GET BACK TO WORK!" Out of nowhere, Howard Fightington jumps in and knocks Benson to the moon! Yeah-yuh!

Fill in the blanks to write your own slacker stories about Mordecai and Rigby.

Mordecai and Rigby are playing _knife glove_ when Benson tells them to _work_. Mordecai asks Benson why he's such a huge _tos_. Uh-oh. Benson's face gets bright red, and he **freaks out** and screams, "_work_!" Out of nowhere, _urhoi_ jumps in and knocks Benson to the moon! Yeah-yuh!

Mordecai and Rigby are playing _H fay hik_
when Benson tells them to _WOTK_.
Mordecai asks Benson why he's such a huge
left. Uh-oh. Benson's face gets
bright red, and he **freaks out** and screams,
"_moGaH_!" Out of nowhere, _he_
jumps in and knocks Benson to the moon!
Yeah-yuh!

Mordecai and Rigby are playing _games_ when
Benson tells them to _____.
Mordecai asks Benson why he's such a huge
_____. Uh-oh. Benson's face gets bright red,
and he **freaks out** and screams, "_____!"
Out of nowhere, _____ jumps in and knocks
Benson to the moon! Yeah-yuh!

One time, Pops had to square off against CrewCrew in a furious rap battle. Do some Rigby-style hamboning (that means slapping your hands against your body to create a killer beat), then write a dope rap below. Make sure it rhymes!

turn around kid it be crime
do i have to go back
in the premises are made for you
so dont step over that line
or else your freind is going to
have a bad time

YOU NEED TO WORK ON YOUR RHYMES, FOOL!

Rigby has a tough-guy alter ego named Fists. Create your own alter ego and give yourself a cool alter-ego name. You can be mean, funny, cool, or even superheroic—whatever you want!

Mordecai and Rigby pranked Muscle Man by giving him a fake million-dollar lottery ticket. What if you won the lottery? What would you do with all that cash? Would you buy a pair of million-dollar pants? Write down your awesome million-dollar ideas on these pages.

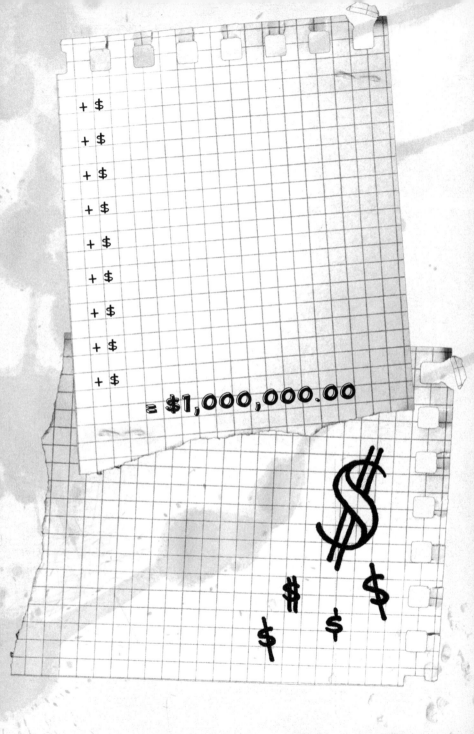

After watching a weirdo British horror movie called **Ello Gov'nor** about an evil taxi, Rigby becomes **terrified** of the evil taxi. He even starts seeing it everywhere!

What are your biggest fears?

If your fears came to life, how would you defeat and destroy them?

One time, the gang had to team up to form a band and save the Park. What if you and your friends formed a band?

What would be the name of your band?

Who would be in it?

What instrument would you play?

What kind of radical outfits would you wear?

Keep a journal for one full week.
Write down anything: stuff that
happens at school, your weird
thoughts, your strange ideas, your
observations, **whatever!**

Monday

Tuesday

Wednesday

Thursday

Friday

Saturday

Sunday

What's YOUR Jam?

Now find the best stuff from your week and use it as material to write some killer lyrics.

And now, a quick tour of the Park!

Muscle Man and Hi Five Ghost's trailer is parked near Pops's house. Those two weirdos live inside.

It's kind of a dump.

Skips's house is also the golf-cart garage. If you had your own golf cart, where would you drive?

no

The Snack Bar is where Park visitors come to chow down. The Snack Bar menu is loaded with delicious junk like ice-cream sandwiches, deep-fried hamburgers, and doughnuts.

Use this page to create your own Snack Bar menu. If you could eat whatever you want, all the time, what would it be? Put it on the menu!

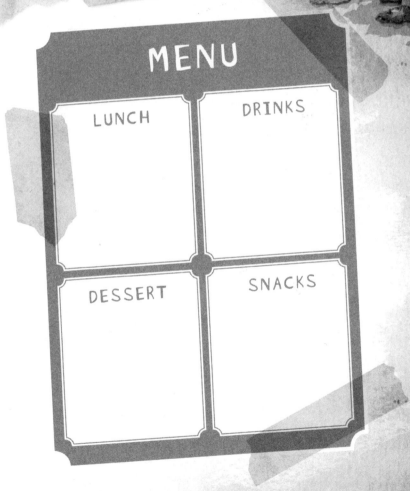

MENU

LUNCH

DRINKS

DESSERT

SNACKS

This is the Playground. One time, Pops sat on a swing and cried for a while. It was super sad.

EVIL HOT DOGS!

Draw more ferocious hot dogs.

But amazingly . . .

Welcome to Pops's House

Mordecai and Rigby live in Pops's house. Sometimes it gets busted up or blown to bits. But it always gets fixed in the end, so it's **all good.**

GOOD SHOW! JOLLY GOOD SHOW!

Pops's house, all
shiny and new!

What if you had an **entire** gigantic house to yourself? Would you let your friends live with you? Would you have one room **just** for video games? Describe your house here.

WHOOO! PARTY!

Now draw it below.

House Rules

Benson has a House Rules book he uses to keep Mordecai and Rigby in line.

No unicorns

No yelling

No harpsichord playing after 10:00 p.m.

No rock-paper-scissors

No feet on the table

No food on the table

No food on the floor

No video games

No overnight camping

No Punchies

No prank calls

No oversize novelty hats on work time

NO VIDEO GAMES?!
ARE YOU NUTS?!

House Rules

What if you could make a
House Rules book for your
house? Write your twelve
most important rules below.

1. _____

2. _____

3. _____

4. _____

5. _____

6. _____

7. _____

8. _____

9. _____

10. _____

11. _____

12. _____

Rigby's favorite song is **Summertime Loving, Loving in the Summer (Time)**. What's your jam? Put on your favorite song and do some journaling, yo.

Why do you like the song so much?

What are your favorite lyrics?

Do you think this will be your favorite song forever?

It's summertime, and I hope you like steak. Gonna take you to a restaurant and eat it at the lake.

Mr. Maellard is Pops's dad and Benson's boss. He's an angry old dude who screams and yells a ton. When you get super angry, what do you yell and scream? Fill in the balloons below with your favorite angry outbursts.

DO IT! OR I'LL YANK THAT BOOK AWAY FROM YOU!

One time, Mordecai saw Pops naked, and he was like, "Aaaarrgghh!" He was all mentally scarred. Have you ever seen or heard something you wanted to forget about so, so, so bad? Write it down here, then scribble all over it. Maybe you'll get lucky and the memory will be erased! But y'know, probably not . . .

FOR REAL, IT WAS GROSS. EVERYTHING WAS ALL SAGGY, WRINKLY, AND PASTY . . .

Scribble over what you write!

Mordecai and Rigby play a ton of video games, even though Rigby stinks at them. What if you could create your own video game? Do it below!

What type of game is it? Sonic and the blak fies

Which console would it be played on? Wii

What's the game's title? Sonic in the borkntre

Does the game's hero have any radical powers? Yes

Describe the final boss. o ween she has 4 souls the dark

I get to be PLAYER ONE!

Draw some super art-school
artistic box art for your game.

Rigby wanted a cool new name, so he tried combining random words. After looking around the room and seeing a bunch of trash and a picture of a boat, he came up with the name Trash Boat.

Come up with your own cool new name. What do you see around you? Find two things, combine them, and that's your new name!

If you need some inspiration, try combining words from the four columns below:

Sandwich	Armpit	Pirate	Funky
Controller	Dancer	Clock	Mug
Chair	Fist	Butt	Sneaker
Cowboy	Lamp	Goggles	Fan

Death is a scary dude. He carries a giant scythe, and one time he tried to take Skips's soul. What if Death came and tried to claim one of your friends' souls? How would you fight him? Would you get a bunch of your other friends to help? Come up with a killer plan to battle Death!

YOUR SOUL IS MINE.

Let's explore the house!

All the video-game action goes down in the **living room**.

The **kitchen** stove can cook up some delicious blueberry pancakes.

Mordecai and Rigby's **bedroom** is always a mess, even though the dudes don't wear clothes. Odd . . .

Describe your bedroom below. Could you make it cooler?

Pops's bedroom

The bathroom

Welcome to the Coffee Shop

Margaret and Eileen work here.

Mordecai and Rigby just hang.

Mordecai and Rigby drink coffee here 'cause Mordecai loves coffee and 'cause he loves Margaret. Do you and your friends have a place you hang out? Describe it here.

_____
_____
_____
_____
_____
_____

The Coffee Shop is home to the arcade game **Broken Bonez**. Draw some arcade-game action on the screen below.

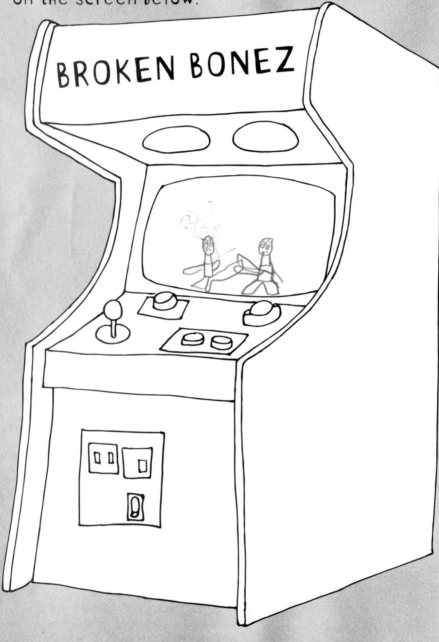

Margaret keeps a diary full of secrets. On the front and back of this page, write down twenty secrets you'd never, ever want anyone to know. When you're done, tear out the page and rip it to shreds so no one learns your secrets!

1.

2.

3.

4.

5.

6.

7.

8.

9.

YOUR SECRETS HAVE TO BE MEANINGFUL!

10.

11.

12.

13.

14.

15.

16.

17.

18.

19.

20.

WEREN'T THERE SECRETS HERE SOMEWHERE?

Doesn't the Coffee Shop look sort of like a school cafeteria?

Write down the absolute **worst** foods your school cafeteria serves for lunch and describe the way they smell in crazy disgusting detail.

If you need some good words for describing the stink, try these:

Odorous	Rancid
Foul	Fetid
Putrid	Garbage-like
Rank	Just plain nasty

I'M GOING TO BARF!

BOSS RUN!

Solve these mazes and destroy the villains before Garrett Bobby Ferguson Jr. unleashes them on the Park!

Yeah-yuh! You nabbed the evil British Taxi!

Can you beat the Hammer? He has one weakness—furniture! Navigate the maze and collect the furniture to destroy him.

You nailed the Hammer!

Make your way through the zoo to defeat
Death Bear. Grab the tranquilizer gun on
the way!

Bear = tranquilized!

Make your way through this final maze and defeat Garrett Bobby Ferguson Jr. before he brings the bad guys back from the grave!

No Rules Guy took Mordecai and Rigby to a magical land where there were **no rules.** What are the first ten things you would do if there were NO RULES?

1.

2.

3.

4.

5.

6.

7.

8.

9.

10.

PSSST. I KNOW a PLACE WHERE RULES DON'T EXIST.

Garrett Bobby Ferguson's beard is missing! Grab a pen and fill it in.
YES, GO AHEAD, DRAW THE BEARD OF GARRETT BOBBY FERGUSON.

What if you were a **crazy evil villain?**
Pretend you are and write all about it below.

What evil powers do you have?

Come up with
a crazy evil
villainous plan to
destroy Mordecai
and Rigby.

After Rigby recites an evil spell in a mirror, he unleashes the demon Ybgir (because **Ybgir** is **Rigby** spelled backward). What's your name spelled backward?

Place this book in front of a mirror and draw an evil demon of your own. But only look at the paper in the mirror while drawing, never look at the actual book. Not as easy as it sounds, is it?

1.

Percy is a super-creepy living doll who is obsessed with drawing on Pops's face. But **you** can draw and write on Pops's face all you want.

Mordecai and Rigby have battled some crazy cool villains. In the space below, draw the most monstrous bad guy you can dream up.

Write On!

Now it's **your turn**. Write your own original story about Mordecai, Rigby, and the rest of the crew!

OR JUST WRITE WHATEVER YOU WANT! IT'S YOUR BOOK! NO RULES!